How big is a giant squid? What is a dragon-fish? How do deep-sea creatures find food? What do scientists think some mythical sea monsters might really be?

Find out the answers to these questions and more in . . .

**Magic Tree House®
Research Guide**

SEA MONSTERS

A nonfiction companion to
Dark Day in the Deep Sea

It's Jack and Annie's very own guide to the strange creatures of the sea.

Including:

• Sea monster legends
• Giant Pacific octopuses
• Prehistoric sea monsters
• Deep-sea exploration

And much more!

Here's what people are saying about the Magic Tree House® Research Guides:

Your Research Guides are a great addition to the Magic Tree House series! I have used Rain Forests *and* Space *as "read-alouds" during science units. Thank you for these!!*—Cheryl M., teacher

My eight-year-old son thinks your books are great—and I agree. I wish my high school students had read the Research Guides when they were his age. —John F., parent and teacher

And from the Magic Tree House® Web site:

My son loves the Research Guides about knights, pirates, and mummies. He has even asked for a notebook, which he takes with him to the museum for his research.—A parent

The Research Guides have been very helpful to us, as our daughter has an abundance of questions. Please come out with more. They help us help her find the answers to her questions!—An appreciative mom and dad

I love your books. I have a great library at home filled with your books and Research Guides. The [Knights and Castles] *Research Guide really helped me do a report on castles and knights!*—A young reader

Magic Tree House®
Research Guide

SEA MONSTERS

A nonfiction companion to
Dark Day in the Deep Sea

by Mary Pope Osborne
and Natalie Pope Boyce

illustrated by Sal Murdocca

A STEPPING STONE BOOK™
Random House New York

Published in the United States by Random House Children's Books,
a division of Random House, Inc., New York.

Random House and colophon are registered trademarks and A Stepping Stone
Book and colophon are trademarks of Random House, Inc. Magic Tree House
is a registered trademark of Mary Pope Osborne; used under license.

Visit us on the Web!
www.magictreehouse.com
www.randomhouse.com/kids

Educators and librarians, for a variety of teaching tools, visit us at
www.randomhouse.com/teachers

Library of Congress Cataloging-in-Publication Data
Osborne, Mary Pope.
Sea monsters / by Mary Pope Osborne and Natalie Pope Boyce ;
illustrated by Sal Murdocca. — 1st ed.
    p.   cm. — (Magic tree house research guide)
"A nonfiction companion to Dark Day in the Deep Sea."
"A Stepping Stone book."
Includes bibliographical references and index.
ISBN 978-0-375-84663-2 (trade) — ISBN 978-0-375-94663-9 (lib. bdg.)
1. Marine animals—Juvenile literature. 2. Marine animals, Fossil—Juvenile
literature. 3. Sea monsters—Juvenile literature. I. Boyce, Natalie Pope.
II. Murdocca, Sal, ill. III. Title.
QL122.2.O83 2008 591.77—dc22 2007012806

Printed in the United States of America
10 9 8 7 6 5 4 3 2 1
First Edition

For Margot Paddock,
and in memory of Skip

Scientific Consultant:

DR. SÖNKE JOHNSEN, Associate Professor, Biology Department, Duke University.

Paleontology Consultant:

DR. ROBERT T. BAKKER.

Education Consultant:

HEIDI JOHNSON, Earth Science and Paleontology, Lowell Junior High School, Bisbee, Arizona.

Very special thanks to Anne Skakel for the excellent photographs; and many thanks to the wonderful team at Random House: Joanne Yates Russell, Gloria Cheng, Mallory Loehr, Angela Roberts, and our great editor, Diane Landolf, whose fine editing skills and encouragement keep us on track every time.

SEA MONSTERS

Contents

Dear Readers,

Sometimes we get frightened when we're in the ocean. It's so dark and mysterious. What if a scary sea monster grabs our feet? We really didn't know much about life deep beneath the sea. So we put our heads together and decided to find out just what lives there. The very best way to learn about anything is to do research. We found out loads of things!

First, we went to the library and found books with lots of pictures of deep-ocean creatures. Then we went online and

found out even more. We actually felt as if we were taking a journey into the ocean! Did you know that there are animals living there that make their own lights? The facts we learned helped us to understand the sea and all its creatures. So dive in and let's begin a new adventure to find out about the amazing animals of the deep sea!

Jack
Annie

1

Sea Monsters

For thousands of years, people have told stories of sea monsters. They have described seeing them in every ocean and even in some lakes.

It is true that there are some scary-looking animals living in the ocean today. Other monstrous-looking sea creatures lived millions of years ago.

Some sea-monster tales may not be true at all. The deep, dark waters of the ocean hold many mysteries. They also hold lots of amazing animals.

Scientists Capture Live Giant Squid
Giant squids are sometimes called "sea monsters." There are stories about giant squids attacking boats and people. But not many people have ever seen one.

Giant squids usually live so deep in the ocean that it is hard to know much about them. Sometimes their bodies wash up on shore, but until recently, no giant squid had ever been seen alive.

In December 2006, scientists were doing research 600 miles off the coast of Japan. They were amazed to catch a live giant squid! The young squid thrashed around wildly as they pulled it into the boat. Sadly, it hurt itself so much that it died. But the scientists are studying the squid to learn more about these rare animals.

Researchers pull up a giant squid, using a smaller squid as bait.

Bigger than *T. rex*!

Long ago, huge sea creatures swam in the oceans. A team of scientists in Canada has found the complete fossil remains of a sea reptile that was seventy-six feet long! That's twice as long as a *Tyrannosaurus rex*!

Snakes, lizards, turtles, and crocodiles are all reptiles. So were dinosaurs!

This animal swam in the oceans more than 25 million years ago. That was long after the dinosaurs had disappeared.

We are beginning to learn more about creatures of the deep. With modern underwater devices, scientists today have new ways of knowing what lies deep within the ocean. And with enough research, they may find out about the animals people call "sea monsters."

World of Monsters

This map of Iceland from the 1500s shows what people 400 years ago imagined the ocean to be like—full of sea monsters!

2

Exploring the Oceans

In December 1872, a ship called the
Challenger sailed from Britain. It was
starting a long three-year voyage. The ship
carried a group of scientists. They planned
to do the first large study of the ocean.
They wanted to see if there was life in the
deep sea. At that time, many people did not
believe there was.

Two men were in charge of the trip. One
was a scientist named Charles Thomson.

The other was Captain George Strong Nares, a naval officer who was an expert in mapmaking.

The men turned the ship into a floating lab. They brought along microscopes, thermometers, chemicals, and hundreds of bottles to hold samples. They also carried gear to collect material from the ocean floor.

The scientists stowed 181 miles of rope on board. That's about as long as the state of Massachusetts is wide!

During the trip, the men took thousands of samples of sea plants and animals. They mapped the ocean floor. They also learned about water temperatures and how salty the water was in different places.

The *Challenger* came back with lots of research material. The voyage proved that the deep ocean had many living creatures. Life in the ocean was richer than anyone had ever dreamed.

Deep-Water Exploration

In 1934, Dr. William Beebe was the first person to dive deep into the sea. He went down 3,000 feet in a vessel called a *bathysphere* (BATH-uh-sfeer). A strong cable lowered it into the water. Since there were no underwater cameras, Dr. Beebe wrote down all he saw. Later, an artist drew pictures of what he described.

Dr. Beebe, left, and his partner, engineer Otis Barton, stand next to the bathysphere.

Things have changed a lot since the *Challenger* and Dr. Beebe. In 1960, a better bathysphere was invented. For the first time, people could dive down to the deepest part of the ocean. They dove seven miles down to the Marianas Trench. No one has ever gone that deep in the ocean before or since.

The Marianas Trench is in the Pacific Ocean off the coast of Japan.

Jacques Cousteau (1910–1997)

When Jacques Cousteau (zhahk koo-STOH) was a young man in France, he had a bad car accident. To get stronger, Jacques swam in the ocean every day. He fell in love with the sea and chose to spend his life studying it.

Jacques invented special underwater cameras and scuba gear. For many years, Jacques made underwater movies and photographs while sailing aboard his famous boat, the *Calypso*. People all over the globe came to know the beautiful world of the ocean.

Jacques wanted everyone to treat the oceans with care. "People protect what they love," he said.

Since Jacques's death, scientists have built new, unmanned submarines. They are able to go deep into the ocean to gather facts. In the future, we will all have a better idea of the wonderful blue world of Jacques Cousteau.

Jacques Cousteau

The Call of the Bloop

In the summer of 1997, scientists made a puzzling discovery. Underwater sensors had picked up very strange sounds. The noises seemed to come from a really huge underwater animal. But just what kind of animal? No animal they knew could make noises like this. The scientists named the mystery creature "the Bloop."

If an animal like the Bloop exists, it is larger than the biggest blue whale. In fact, if this animal exists, it might be the largest animal on earth! But to this day, no one has a clue about what the Bloop really is. The strange sounds have never been heard again.

3

Squids, Octopuses, and Other Creatures

Most *marine* animals we know about live near the surface of the ocean. But many other creatures live deep beneath the sea.

Marine comes from the Latin word mare, which means "sea."

Sometimes an animal often called a "sea monster" swims up to the surface from its home in the deep. This scary-looking animal is known as the giant squid.

Giant Squids

There are many kinds of squids, but the *giant squid* is one of the largest. Because giant squids live deep in the sea, we do not know a lot about them.

Squids are <u>invertebrates</u> (in-VUR-tuh-brayts). Invertebrates do not have a backbone.

Feeding tentacles

2 rows of suckers

Arms

Large eye

Mantle

Parrot-like beak and mouth

Head

Siphon

Stabilizing fins

We do know that giant squids have huge heads and eyes. They have strong, hard beaks, eight arms, and two tentacles. The tentacles are much longer than the arms. They can grow to over thirty feet long! Powerful suckers lined with teeth cover each arm. The tentacles have suckers only at the ends.

This close-up shows an arm with its two rows of suckers.

The Biggest Eyes

Giant squids have the largest eyes in the animal kingdom. Their eyes are about fifteen inches wide. Think soccer balls or basketballs! Giant squids need their large eyes to see in the dark, deep water.

Catching Prey

Squids are *carnivores* (KAR-nuh-vorz), or meat-eaters. Giant squids eat marine animals, but experts are not sure exactly what kind.

They catch their prey with their tentacles. Then they coil their arms around their victim just like a python.

Finally, giant squids bite their prey into pieces with their powerful beaks. They have a bony tongue called a *radula* (RAA-juh-luh). The radula has many tiny teeth on it. These teeth break the food down into even smaller bits.

Squid beaks look a lot like parrot beaks.

Movement

Giant squids can move as fast as twenty-three miles an hour. When they move quickly, they spurt water from a *siphon* (SY-fun) in their mantles. They take water in and then shoot it out.

The force of the water pushes the squids where they want to go. Squids use their strong fins to move forward toward their food.

Colossal Squids

For many years, scientists thought that giant squids were the largest squids. But in 1925, scientists found some tentacles in a sperm whale's stomach. These tentacles were different from the giant squid's. They came from a squid that was even larger!

34

Scientists named this squid the *colossal* (kuh-LAH-sul) *squid*. Since then, other tentacles have been found in whales. Fishermen have also pulled up parts of colossal squids' bodies.

Colossal means "really enormous"! Huge! Gigantic!

A Great Find

In 2003, fishermen spotted a colossal squid feeding off the coast of Antarctica. They managed to haul it into their boat. It, too, died when they got it on board.

It is rare to see the entire body of a colossal squid. Scientists found that it had two huge beaks and small teeth that looked like a parrot's. Sharp hooks on its arms turned in circles. Its body was wider and fatter than the giant squid's. But we still aren't certain how long colossal squids grow to be.

The Squids and the Whales

Sperm whales feed on all kinds of squids, even the biggest. In fact, some sperm whales have been found to have more than 15,000 squid beaks in their stomachs!

Sperm whales can grow up to fifty feet long. They dive very deep into the ocean and can hold their breath for two hours! No one has ever seen a sperm whale fight a giant or colossal squid. But scientists often see scars on the whales' skin that were made by the squids' suckers. Imagine what a battle *that* must have been!

New Squid Discovered

In 2001, underwater cameras filmed a very weird squid. No one had ever seen anything like it.

An expert from the National Museum of Natural History studied the film. He saw an animal with a tiny body and ten long arms, each about twenty-three feet.

But the most unusual thing about this squid was its two large fins. They flapped around its small body just like elephant ears!

Octopus comes from a Greek word that means "eight-footed."

Octopuses

There are many different kinds of octopuses in oceans around the world. Octopuses come in all sizes. The largest are the giant Pacific octopuses. Their arms grow to be fourteen to sixteen feet long.

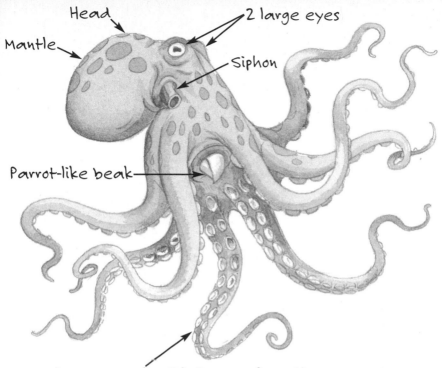

Head

2 large eyes

Mantle

Siphon

Parrot-like beak

8 arms, each with 2 rows of suction cups on the undersides

Unlike squids, octopuses do not have tentacles. They have eight arms with two rows of suckers on each arm. Each sucker has a taste bud on it. The arms can move in any direction. Octopuses taste whatever they touch. If they lose an arm, that's no problem—they will grow another!

Most of the time, octopuses crawl or walk over the ocean floor. But just like squids, they can move quickly by shooting water from their mantle.

Big Brains

Some octopuses look dangerous. Actually, most are very shy. They seem to have their own personalities. They also seem to be curious. Sometimes they will touch divers in a gentle way, almost as if they were exploring or tasting them.

Wait! There is one dangerous octopus—the blue-ringed octopus. Its poison will kill a human in seconds! It's only as big as an egg!

Octopuses have large brains shaped like doughnuts. Their brains wrap around their throats. They are as smart as dogs!

One night at the Seattle Aquarium, an octopus crawled out of its tank. It slipped into other tanks and ate some fish. Then it went back home. The next morning, the octopus's keeper found a wet trail on the floor.

Some octopuses can unscrew caps from bottles. An octopus named Frida lived in

This octopus opens plastic Easter eggs filled with shrimp!

a German zoo. By watching her keepers, Frida learned to open a can of shrimp. She even put on a "can opening" show for visitors.

Some octopuses seem to play in the bubbles coming from air tubes in their tanks. One octopus spread her mantle and "surfed" on the tide of bubbles!

Making a Home

Octopuses live in dens under rocks or in cracks on the ocean floor. For protection, they pile rocks outside the openings.

One scientist watched an octopus catch some fish. Before eating, the octopus shoved rocks up in front of itself to make a fort. Then it settled down to eat.

Octopuses lay eggs in their dens and tend them for up to six months until they hatch. The giant Pacific octopus lays over 57,000 eggs! Each egg is the size of a grain of rice. Out of all these eggs, only a few will survive.

The female giant Pacific octopus lives from three to five years and dies shortly after her eggs hatch.

Self-Defense

Octopuses trick their enemies by quickly changing their skin color. They turn the same color as the background. When an animal's skin matches its background, we say it is using *camouflage* (KAA-muh-flahj).

When octopuses are in danger, they shoot a stream of black ink into the water. The ink clouds up the water. It stings predators' eyes and confuses their sense of smell. The octopus turns white and slips away. The predator thinks it is still hiding in the cloud of ink.

Night Hunters

Octopuses are *nocturnal* (nok-TUR-null) hunters. This means they mainly hunt at night.

Octopuses eat fish, lobsters, clams, snails, crabs, turtles, shrimp, and scallops. If an animal has a hard shell, the octopus bites it with its beak to try and open it. Sometimes it will bite right through the

 A giant Pacific octopus feasts on a spiny dogfish.

shell. Then the octopus shoots out a poison that stuns its prey. Soon the muscle that holds the shell together dissolves, and the octopus can tear it apart.

Octopuses
Eight arms
Big brains
Live in dens or cracks
Squirt ink
Change color

Mystery at the Aquarium
At the Seattle Aquarium, sand sharks lived in a large tank with other animals. There was one problem. Their keepers kept finding the sharks' dead bodies at the bottom of the tank. No one could figure out why. To solve the mystery, they put a video camera in the tank.

The camera showed a shark swimming around. Suddenly a giant Pacific octopus attacked from behind a rock. The octopus wrapped its arms around the shark and held it in a deadly grip. Even though the shark struggled, it was no use. The next day, there was another dead shark in the tank.

I guess sharks and giant Pacific octopuses don't make good roommates!

The Fierce Little Walnut

The female blanket octopus grows to over six feet long. Recently divers off the coast of Australia captured a live male blanket octopus. Male blanket octopuses are almost never seen. That's because they are just under an inch long! That's as big as a walnut.

This tiny male defends himself with weapons! He grabs two tentacles from a passing jellyfish. When predators approach, he waves the stinging tentacles in their faces! Whoaaa! Back off, buddy!

The male blanket octopus is only nine-tenths of an inch long.

Manta Rays

Imagine diving around a coral reef. Suddenly a huge creature appears overhead. The monster has two large black wings that flap as it moves. It also has horns and a big, long mouth.

This animal is not really a monster. It is a manta ray, or devilfish. Manta rays can

Manta ray

reach sixteen feet in length and weigh over two tons. As they swim, their wings gently flap up and down. The wings are actually fins.

Manta rays' bodies are shaped like diamonds. Their shape helps them glide easily through the water. Manta rays swim with their mouths open to catch any *plankton* floating by. Their horns push the plankton toward their mouths.

Plankton are tiny plants and animals that float in the water. Many sea creatures eat plankton.

Even though manta rays look scary, they are not poisonous. They are called "devilfish" only because of their horns.

Steve Irwin and the Stingray

Stingrays are close relatives of manta rays. Stingrays are only about two feet long. They have poisonous, sharp barbs on their tails. Because stingrays are flat, they can hide easily beneath the sand.

 Steve Irwin and his daughter, Bindi Sue, pet a Bengal tiger cub.

A stingray caused the death of Steve Irwin. Steve was a wildlife expert known as the "Crocodile Hunter." He had a popular television show about animals. When Steve was filming in the ocean near Australia, he startled a stingray. The ray lashed out with its tail. Its barb hit Steve right in the heart. He died within seconds. It was a terrible accident. Stingrays are not usually dangerous to people.

Giant Mekong Catfish

For thousands of years, monster fish have lived in the Mekong River in Thailand. Giant Mekong catfish are the largest freshwater fish in the world. Some grow to the size of grizzly bears. Mekong catfish don't have any teeth.

People living along the river honor them as sacred and special beings.

In 2005, Thai fishermen pulled in a giant catfish. It weighed 646 pounds and was almost nine feet long! That's the

51

160107

biggest catfish anyone has ever seen. The fish fought for over an hour until fishermen finally pulled it in. That night, lots of happy families had catfish for dinner.

 Two people had to hold the 646-pound catfish for this picture.

Giant Jellyfish Invade Japan

Thousands of huge Nomura's jellyfish have crowded into the waters off Japan. These jellyfish get to be six feet wide and can weigh over 450 pounds!

Jellyfish are not really fish, so some scientists call them <u>jellies</u>.

It is rare to die from a jellyfish sting. But if you ever get one, wash it with salt water and then put vinegar on the wound.

Besides stinging people, the jellyfish clog up fishing nets and kill fish with their poisonous stings. The fishermen are not happy!

Jellyfish live in waters around the world. They have soft bodies and trailing tentacles, sometimes hundreds of them. Jellyfish use their tentacles to catch fish. Each one is armed with stinging, poisonous cells.

You might be surprised to know that the *longest* animal in the world is not a whale. It is a special jellyfish called a *siphonophore* (sy-FON-uh-for). Its tentacles can reach 131 feet long!

Our ideas about sea monsters seem a little less scary when we know the facts. Squids, octopuses, and all the sea creatures that frighten us are not monsters. They're just surprising and wonderful animals!

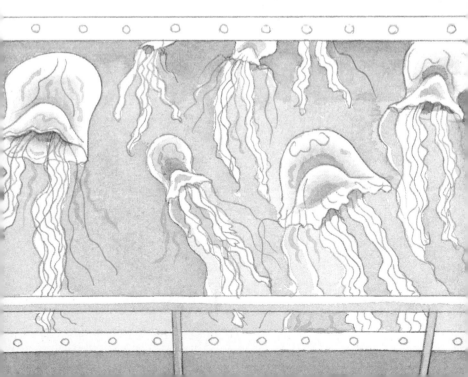

Mystery Globster

In 1993, a huge mass of jelly-like flesh washed up on the shore of Chile. It had no head or bones. The mass was forty-one feet long and nineteen feet wide.

Scientists call unknown remains on beaches "globsters." This globster caused a lot of excitement. No one knew what it was. Was it a new creature? Even the scientists were stumped. They said, "It doesn't look like a dead whale." And then they said, "It doesn't smell like a dead whale."

After lots more testing, the mystery was solved. Guess what? It was a dead whale.

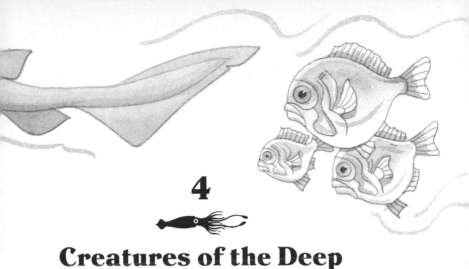

4

Creatures of the Deep

When we go 3,000 feet into the ocean, there is almost no sunlight. Weird shapes sometimes glide by in the murky water. Some seem to have no color. They are so clear, you can see right through them. Others swim by with shiny silver scales that reflect light. Many animals even have lights shining from their bodies.

In the very deepest part of the ocean, there is no sunlight at all. Scientists call

Abyss comes from a Greek word meaning "bottomless."

this the *abyss* (uh-BIS). At its deepest, the abyss goes down over 35,000 feet! It is pitch-black and very cold—just above freezing.

Most of the ocean lies 12,000 feet below the surface. The deep ocean makes up about 60 percent of the earth's surface. It is an exciting and awesome place. There are live volcanoes oozing glowing lava. There are gigantic mountains, bigger than any on the land. And there are trenches almost too deep to measure.

Exploring the Deep

People have just begun to explore the deep ocean. If they tried to dive to the bottom, the weight of all that water would crush them. This used to be true of underwater cameras, too. But today there are unmanned mini-subs that can carry cameras deep underwater. As a result, scientists are discovering sea creatures that they never knew existed.

This crab is almost as large as the mini-sub!

Life in the Deep Ocean

There is not much for animals to eat in the deep ocean. Some animals swim to the surface for food. Others wait for scraps to float down to the bottom. But most lurk in the dark, waiting for prey.

In order to capture animals larger than themselves, many deep-sea creatures have huge jaws and big teeth. Gulper eels are almost all mouth. They wait until another fish swims by. Then they open their mouths really wide. Their mouths look like an open umbrella.

Gulper eels are also called "umbrella eels."

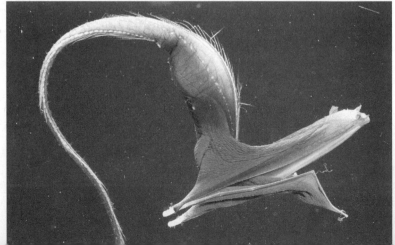

Since there is little light, many deep-sea animals have small eyes. But others have really huge eyes that help them see better in the dark.

Jewel squids have one eye bigger than the other. One looks up; the other looks down.

Bioluminescence

Even though the abyss is very dark, flashing lights sometimes light up the dark. They come from the animals that live there.

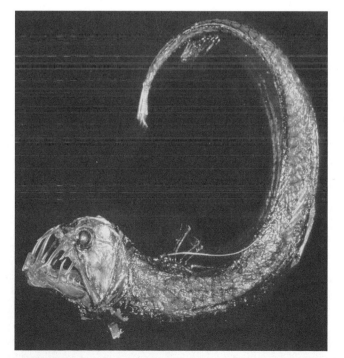

Viperfish have over 350 lights in their mouths.

Most marine creatures in the deep ocean make their own lights. This is called *bioluminescence* (by-oh-loo-min-ESS-ense). The light comes from organs on their bodies called *photophores* (FOE-tuh-forz). Photophores create light that is almost always light blue. But some animals produce yellow, green, or red lights.

Bioluminescence is used for:
1. Finding a mate
2. Confusing predators
3. Communication
4. Attracting prey

Vampire Squids

Vampire squids look a little like squids or octopuses. In fact, they are neither. They are one of a kind. These strange creatures live in the deep ocean.

Although vampire squids are small, their looks are chilling. They have strong white beaks, big red eyes, and black bodies. Their eight arms are connected to each other by webbed skin covered in photophores.

Cape Tricks

When they are in danger, vampire squids whip their arms over their head. They look like they're wearing a vampire's cape. This makes them look bigger than they really are.

Then vampire squids quickly flap

If you touched the tip of their arms, bright blue lights would flash.

their arms up and down. This creates flashing lights that dazzle and confuse their predators.

Vampire squids drop down over their victims like a net. If that sounds scary, keep in mind that this is a little creature. You'll probably never see it. And if you do, it is harmless to people.

Anglerfish

Have you ever seen fish with built-in fishing poles? *Anglerfish* are a kind of fish that fish! Many types of anglerfish live in the deep ocean. They don't grow very large, but they look really scary.

Angler is another word for "fisherman."

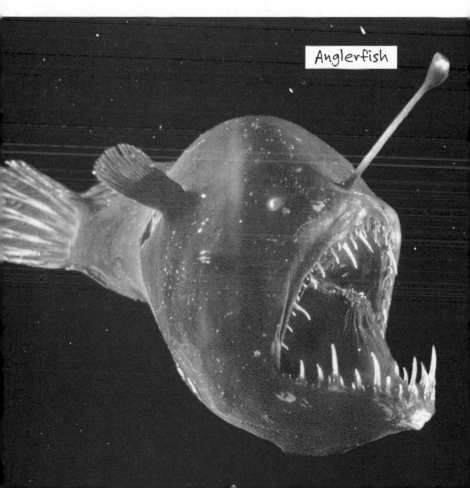

Anglerfish

Anglerfish have heads much bigger than their bodies. Their mouths are filled with wicked-looking teeth. In fact, many anglerfish can't even close their mouths because of their teeth.

Their fishing poles grow right out of their heads. They glow with a bluish light. The poles have a growth at the end of them that looks like bait. When the anglerfish wiggle their poles, other fish think the growths are prey.

As the curious fish swim closer, the anglerfish snaps them up! Anglerfish have teeth that go right down into their throats. The teeth act like traps. No prey ever escapes the deadly anglerfish!

Male anglerfish are tiny compared to females. When the male finds a female, he bites her on the back. Then he lives on her for the rest of his life.

Females lay eggs that come out in a clear sheet about twenty-five feet long and three feet wide.

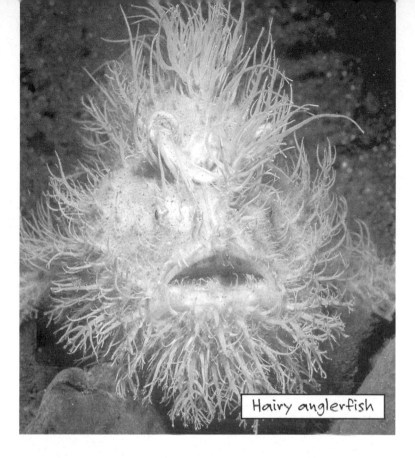

Hairy anglerfish

Is It a Beach Ball?

No, it's a hairy anglerfish! Hairy anglerfish are as round as beach balls. They have *antennas* (an-TEN-uhz) sprouting out all over their bodies. These antennas are sense organs that help them find prey.

Dragonfish

Dragonfish are small but terrible-looking creatures. They have big heads and a mouth full of wicked, fang-like teeth.

Here is a dragonfish with its long barbel.

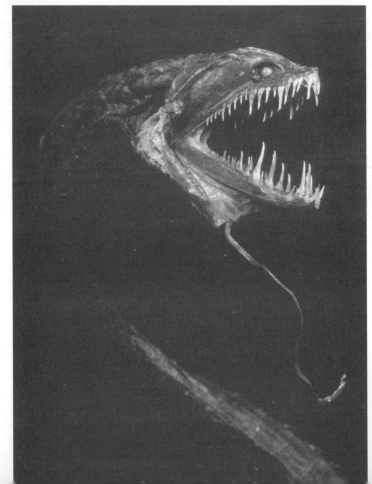

Hanging from their mouths are thin lines called *barbels* (BAR-bulz). Barbels can hang down over six feet! Lighted lures cover their tips.

In addition to barbels, some dragonfish have photophores behind their eyes. Scientists wonder if they use them like spotlights. No one is sure exactly how dragonfish behave. Only a few have ever been seen alive in the ocean.

Oarfish

Oarfish are often mistaken for giant sea snakes. They also look like long . . . *very* long ribbons. In fact, one kind of these shiny, silvery fish is fifty feet long!

Some experts believe that oarfish can live with only half a body.

They live deep below the surface and are rarely seen.

A red crest runs from their heads

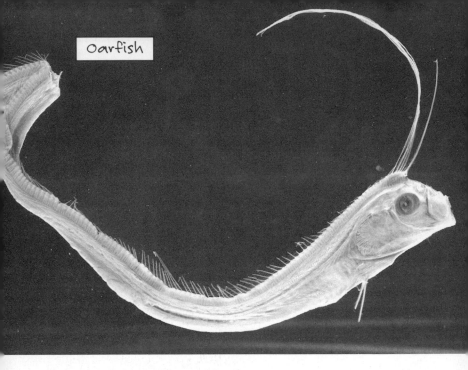

Oarfish

down their bodies. Oarfish sometimes wash up on beaches or swim to the surface when they are sick or dying.

Pink Goblins and Cookie-Cutters

Most sharks live near the surface. However, some very unusual sharks live in the deep ocean.

Among these are goblin sharks. *Goblin* means "evil spirit." Goblin sharks are not evil spirits. They're very strange sharks with long, pointed snouts jutting out over their mouths. When goblin sharks catch something, their jaws push forward and open quickly.

Another unusual thing about goblin sharks is their color. They're pinkish gray.

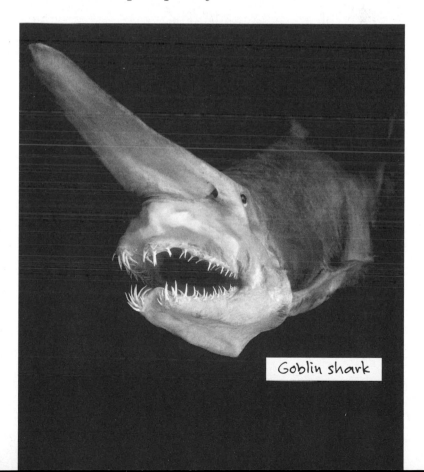

Goblin shark

Cookie-cutter sharks give off blue lights as they swim. The lights cover their lower body and match the light from above. Because of this, predators below can't see cookie-cutter sharks.

The most unusual thing about these sharks is the circular bites they take out of other animals. They take bites out of dolphins, whales, squids, and other marine animals.

Cookie-cutter sharks have even left their marks on submarines!

Cookie-cutter sharks have round mouths. When they bite something, they twist and turn their bodies around and around. By doing this, they cut perfectly round holes into their victims, just like a cookie-cutter.

Some creatures of the deep sea may seem strange. They may even look like monsters. But they are just really exciting animals. We have explored only a tiny part of the deep ocean. There is so much more to find in this dark and wonderful world.

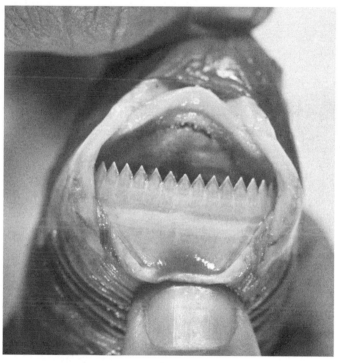

This shows the round mouth and sharp teeth of the cookie-cutter shark.

Giant Tube Worms

New sea floor starts out as hot, flowing rock from deep within the earth. The melted rocks heat up the water to over 700 degrees Fahrenheit. That's super hot!

Giant tube worms live by hot water openings in the Pacific Ocean. These colorful creatures have bright red plumes. They look like tubes of lipstick.

Tube worms have no mouths or insides. They live on bacteria that grow in their bodies. The bacteria change chemicals in the water into food for the worms. Tube worms grow really fast—about thirty-three inches a year. Imagine if you grew that fast. Just like a tube worm, you'd be over eight feet tall in no time!

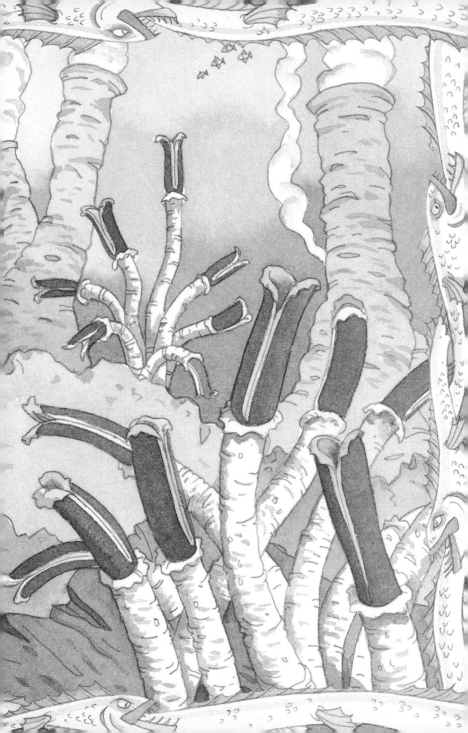

5

Prehistoric Seas

Millions of years ago, amazing animals lived in the oceans. They lived during *prehistoric times*. Prehistoric times came before anyone could write down what went on in the world.

Many of these incredible animals lived in the *Mesozoic Era* (mes-uh-ZOH-ick EHR-uh), which began 251 million years ago. We call this time the "Age of Reptiles."

The Mesozoic lasted for about 180 million years. There were no humans on earth yet. But during this time and even before, fierce animals lived on the earth and in the seas. Much of what we know about them comes from their fossils.

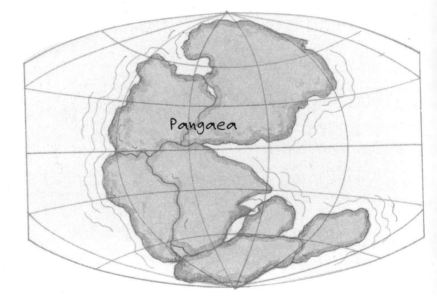

 The earth 250 million years ago.

There was just one huge continent when the Mesozoic Era began. It is called *Pangaea* (pan-JEE-uh). Over millions of years, it broke apart into the continents we know today.

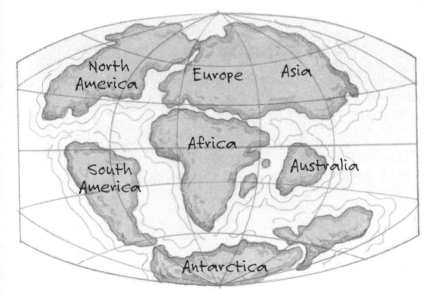

The earth 70 million years ago.

At this time, the earth was much warmer. There was little or no ice at the North and South Poles. The seas were higher. They covered much of the land that exists today. Giant ferns and flowering plants grew in the warm climate. Dinosaurs roamed the earth. Large winged reptiles flew in the skies overhead. Huge, dragon-like reptiles, monstrous sharks, and other scary creatures filled the ocean.

Reptiles of the Sea
The marine reptiles that lived in the ancient seas were not dinosaurs. They were more closely related to lizards and snakes.

Dinosaurs ruled the land, but giant marine reptiles ruled the seas. Many had enormous bodies, heads, and teeth. They were deadly hunters, often moving at fast speeds.

When you see the fossils of ancient sea creatures, you can hardly believe your eyes. Never in your wildest dreams could animals be so huge and scary!

Dunkleosteus (dun-kul-OS-tee-us)

Dunkleosteus was part of a family whose name means "terrible fish." And they were really *TERRIBLE*! These twenty-foot-long predators lived about 400 million years ago—long before the Mesozoic Era.

Dunkleosteus had the strongest jaws of any fish ever. If this monster bit you, 8,000 pounds of pressure per square inch would crush you like a bug. In fact, *Dunkleosteus* could cut a big shark cleanly in half!

You might think an animal this fierce had huge teeth. But *Dunkleosteus* didn't have real teeth. Instead, it had two long, sharp, bony blades. The front of the jawbones came to a fang-like point.

Their mouths opened in a flash and sucked their prey right in. And guess what? Fossils show that *Dunkleosteus* threw up a lot as well. Fossil lumps of half-eaten prey appear to come from these terrible fish. It seems they ate many things that they couldn't digest.

These pictures show our size next to the prehistoric creature's size.

Liopleurodon (ly-uh-PLUH-ruh-don)
Yikes! Talk about colossal! This was the biggest carnivore ever. *Liopleurodon* could be over eighty feet long! Imagine an animal longer than the biggest trucks on the highway. Imagine an animal twenty times heavier than a *T. rex*.

These Mesozoic creatures had long bodies with two flippers on each side. Their huge heads were over ten feet long, bigger than many cars. They had super-strong jaws with powerful eight-inch teeth shaped like tigers' fangs. *Liopleurodon* used their noses to smell prey underwater. Imagine if one of these monsters got a whiff of you!

Elasmosaurus (ih-laaz-muh-SAW-rus)

Elasmosaurus looks like a mistake. Nothing with such a small head could have a neck this long! Picture an animal that is forty-six feet long, and half of its body is its neck! The neck was made up of seventy vertebrae (VUR-tuh-bray), or back bones.

Elasmosaurus ate squid and fish. It may have used its long neck to sweep the ocean floor for crabs and fish. Plus, it swallowed rocks. Piles of rocks are found in the stomachs of *Elasmosaurus* fossils. Maybe the stones helped grind up shells. Crocodiles swallow rocks to do this today.

When fossils of *Elasmosaurus* were first discovered over one hundred years ago, a famous scientist named Edward Drinker Cope put them together. But he made a big mistake. He put the head on the tail end instead of on the neck!

When his mistake was discovered, Cope spent the rest of his life feeling bad about it—even though he was one of the best prehistoric marine-reptile experts of his day.

Xiphactinus (zuh-FACK-tuh-nus)

Xiphactinus is nicknamed the "bulldog fish." Its lower jaws jut out, showing rows of terrible sharp teeth. But another name for these big fish could be "speedy."

Xiphactinus swam really fast. Their powerful tails helped them reach speeds up to thirty-five miles per hour!

Xiphactinus sometimes grew up to twenty feet long. Scientists have found their fossils with much bigger animals inside their stomachs. Thanks to those fierce jaws and teeth, these bulldog fish weren't afraid of anything!

Megalodon (MEG-uh-loh-don)

Sometimes people find giant sharks' teeth along the Maryland, North Carolina, and California coasts. They're as big as dinner plates! The teeth belonged to a huge shark called *Megalodon*, which means "giant tooth." These massive sharks lived after the Mesozoic Era had ended.

There are almost no fossils of *Megalodon* skulls and skeletons. That's because shark skeletons are made of *cartilage* (KAR-tuh-lidge), not bone. Cartilage rots after the animal dies. But teeth turn into long-lasting fossils.

We know by their teeth that *Megalodon* were three times bigger than great white sharks. It's possible they reached over fifty feet long! Their jaws could open over seven feet high and six feet wide.

An animal this size could wolf down a whole cow in one gulp! It could eat a class of third graders in three gulps! But we know that *Megalodon* ate whales instead. Fossils of whale skeletons have been found with cut marks on their ribs and fins. The cuts match *Megalodon* teeth. And right next to the whale fossils were *Megalodon* teeth!

6

Sea-Monster Tales

People have believed in sea monsters for thousands of years. Prehistoric people painted strange sea creatures on the walls of caves. Later, the ancient Greeks had a sea-monster goddess named Keto, who ruled over all the other sea monsters.

Over the years, hundreds of people worldwide have reported spotting sea monsters. Even today, crowds visit Scotland trying to see Nessie, a famous sea monster who is said to live in a lake there.

People who say they have seen sea monsters describe them in different ways. Some say they looked like awful sea serpents. Others say they had long arms to drag ships to the bottom of the sea.

One man reported seeing a huge monster with lots of feet and long hair growing out of its nose.

Some sailors spotted a monster with "glaring eyes" and a body like a lion.

Eyewitness to a Monster

In 1734, the missionary Hans Egede was on a boat headed for Greenland. Suddenly he heard people shouting. Hans looked up and saw "a terrible sea-animal." He wrote that the monster had a lower body "like a snake" and "blew like a whale."

The monster's head was taller than the

This illustration was based on Hans Egede's description.

sails. When it slipped back into the water, Hans saw that it was as long as the boat.

Kraken

About 500 years ago, a writer described monsters living off the coasts of Norway and Iceland.

He called them *kraken*. The writer claimed kraken were as big as islands. They were so strong, they could pull warships down to the ocean bottom.

There are many other stories about kraken attacks on ships and people. Sailors claimed the kraken created deadly whirlpools when they dove down into the water.

A kraken attacks a ship in this illustration from around 1700.

Some said the kraken looked like giant lobsters or crabs. Others reported the kraken were large whales. Then everyone seemed to agree that the kraken looked like an octopus. Kraken legends spread all over the world.

Today scientists think that maybe the kraken were really giant squids. They wonder if the squids mistook the boats for prey. Imagine being a sailor long ago in a small boat. If you saw the mighty tentacles of a giant squid, you might call it a sea monster.

The Jules Verne Race

A long time ago, Jules Verne wrote a book about a giant squid attacking a boat. The book was called *20,000 Leagues Under the Sea*. Jules Verne also wrote a book about a race called *Around the World in Eighty Days*. Both books became very famous.

 This is a scene from the original 1870 French edition of <u>20,000 Leagues Under the Sea</u>.

In 2003, a sailboat was in a race around the world. The race was called the Jules

Verne Race. Suddenly the crew felt something hit the boat. They looked down. To their horror, they saw huge tentacles pulling at the bottom of the boat. One sailor said the tentacles were as big as a man's leg. They belonged to a giant squid!

Quickly, the crew stopped the boat. The squid slipped back into the water. Everyone was in awe that this happened in a race named after Jules Verne. Could a squid like this be what Hans Egede saw as well?

Lusca

People in the *Caribbean* (kare-uh-BEE-un) *Islands* tell tales of a sea monster called the lusca. It is said to be half-shark, half-octopus. Some stories say it is

The Caribbean Islands are in the Atlantic Ocean off the coast of Central America.

101

over seventy-five feet long. According to legend, the lusca makes its home in underwater caves in the ocean.

People believe that the lusca's breath creates underwater currents. When it breathes in, water fills the caves. When it breathes out, fresh water rushes to the surface. Some stories say the lusca can change color.

Many scientists wonder if the lusca might really be an octopus. They say its ability to change color is like that of an octopus. They also know that octopuses eat animals that often live in underwater caves.

Sea Serpents in the Headlines

In 1817, the town of Gloucester (GLOSS-tur), Massachusetts, was in an uproar. Everyone was alarmed about a strange sea serpent swimming in the harbor. Many who saw it described the monster as brown and about forty feet long. Its head was bigger than a dog's but looked like a turtle's. It had a horn on its head. It swam the same way a caterpillar moves.

The sea serpent returned many times. As many as 200 people gathered on the shore to see this amazing sight.

Some even followed it in boats and shot at it.

Finally, the sightings stopped. Life returned to normal. But no one ever knew what the creature really was.

This is an 1817 illustration of the monster in Gloucester.

In 1848, a British naval ship was in the South Atlantic. Suddenly a huge animal over sixty feet long with a mane on its head rose above the water.

Stories of a monster sea serpent once again filled all the newspapers. And once again, nobody ever found out what the animal really was.

 This illustration of the sighting is from the 1883 book <u>Sea Monsters Unmasked</u>.

Nessie

Thousands of years ago, fierce tribes lived around a lake in Scotland called Loch Ness. They carved all kinds of animals into stone. One animal they carved looked like a strange swimming creature.

Loch is the Scottish word for "lake."

As the years passed, hundreds of people have reported seeing an animal like this in the lake. They named it Nessie.

In 1943, a soldier spotted Nessie about 250 yards offshore. He said that she had a long body and neck. Her neck stayed out of the water as she swam. Other people reported seeing the same thing.

 This photo of Nessie is a famous hoax.

Over the years, people have taken photos of Nessie. Many have proven to be fakes. Most are very blurry. One man confessed he made a Nessie out of clay and attached it to a toy submarine. The submarine pulled "Nessie" around the lake while he took pictures.

Finally, in 2003, scientists put 600 sonar devices into the lake. They were supposed to record Nessie sounds. But there were no strange sounds to record. The scientists decided that Nessie does not exist at all.

Still, lots of people are convinced there is something in Loch Ness. After all, so many people have spotted Nessie.

Do Sea Monsters Exist?

What do you think? We think that's a hard question to answer. We know that people really saw something in Gloucester Harbor. And for thousands of years, people have seen many strange and scary things in the ocean.

There are hundreds of stories about sea serpents. Do you think these creatures could be giant oarfish or squids? The truth is that no one really knows exactly what they are.

The mystery lies within the seas. And until we can fully explore this mysterious world, we just don't have all the answers.

The oceans are so vast and deep. We fear what we cannot see or understand. Maybe it's our fear that creates monsters in the deep . . . or anywhere else.

Doing More Research

There's a lot more you can learn about sea monsters. The fun of research is seeing how many different sources you can explore.

Books

Most libraries and bookstores have lots of books about creatures of the deep.

Here are some things to remember when you're using books for research:

1. You don't have to read the whole book. Check the table of contents and the index to find the topics you're interested in.

2. Write down the name of the book.
When you take notes, make sure you write down the name of the book in your notebook so you can find it again.

3. Never copy exactly from a book.
When you learn something new from a book, put it in your own words.

4. Make sure the book is <u>nonfiction</u>.
Some books tell make-believe stories about sea creatures. Make-believe stories are called *fiction*. They're fun to read, but not good for research.

Research books have facts and tell true stories. They are called *nonfiction*. A librarian or teacher can help you make sure the books you use for research are nonfiction.

Here are some good nonfiction books about sea creatures:

- *Deep Sea Adventures* by Kirsten Hall

- *Dive! A Book of Deep-Sea Creatures* by Melvin Berger

- *Encyclopedia Prehistorica: Sharks and Other Sea Monsters* by Robert Sabuda and Matthew Reinhart

- *Giant Squid: Mystery of the Deep* by Jennifer Dussling

- *Octopuses and Squids* by Mary Jo Rhodes and David Hall

- *Outside and Inside Giant Squid* by Sandra Markle

- *Real-Life Sea Monsters* by Judith Jango-Cohen

Museums and Aquariums

Many museums and aquariums have exhibits on sea monsters. These places can help you learn more about the deep sea and the animals that live there.

When you go to a museum or aquarium:

1. Be sure to take your notebook!
Write down anything that catches your interest. Draw pictures, too!

2. Ask questions.
There are almost always people at museums and aquariums who can help you find what you're looking for.

3. Check the museum or aquarium calendar.
Many museums and aquariums have special events and activities just for kids!

Here are some museums and aquariums with exhibits about the deep sea:

- American Museum of Natural History, New York City, New York
- Denver Museum of Nature & Science, Denver, Colorado
- Museum of the Rockies, Bozeman, Montana
- New England Aquarium, Boston, Massachusetts
- Seattle Aquarium, Seattle, Washington
- Shedd Aquarium, Chicago, Illinois

Videos and DVDs

There are some great nonfiction videos and DVDs about sea monsters. As with books, make sure the videos and DVDs you watch for research are nonfiction!

Check your library or video store for these and other nonfiction titles about sea monsters:

- *The Beast of Loch Ness*
  from PBS

- *Ocean Drifters*
  from National Geographic

- *Paleo World: Sea Monsters*
  from Discovery Channel

- *Sea Monsters: A Prehistoric Adventure*
  from National Geographic Giant Screen Films

- *Sea Monsters: Search for the Giant Squid*
  from National Geographic

The Internet

Many Web sites have lots of facts about sea monsters. Some also have games and activities that can help make learning about the deep sea even more fun.

Ask your teacher or your parents to help you find more Web sites like these:

- www.discover.com/issues/oct-03/ features/feateye/

- www.enchantedlearning.com/coloring/ oceanlife.shtml/

- www.livescience.com/animalworld/ 051209_sea_monsters.html

- http://nationalzoo.si.edu/support/ adoptspecies/animalinfo/giantoctopus/ default.cfm

- http://news.bbc.co.uk/cbbcnews/hi/
  animals/newsid_2915000/2915281.stm

- http://news.nationalgeographic.com/
  news/2003/04/0423_030423_
  seamonsters.html

- www.nwf.org/nationalwildlife/
  article.cfm?issueID=9&articleID=62

- www.teachers.ash.org.au/jmresources/
  deep/creatures.html

Good luck!

Index

Photos courtesy of:

If you're looking forward to
Eve of the Emperor Penguin,
you'll love finding out the facts
behind the fiction in

Magic Tree House® Research Guide

PENGUINS AND ANTARCTICA

A nonfiction companion to
Eve of the Emperor Penguin

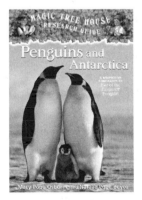

It's Jack and Annie's very own guide to
the world of the Antarctic!

Look for it September 2008!

Magic Tree House® Books

Other books by Mary Pope Osborne:

Picture books:

The Brave Little Seamstress

Happy Birthday, America

Kate and the Beanstalk

Mo and His Friends

Moonhorse

New York's Bravest

Pompeii: Lost and Found

Rocking Horse Christmas

Sleeping Bobby by Mary Pope Osborne and
    Will Osborne

First chapter books:

The Magic Tree House® series

For middle-grade readers:

Adaline Falling Star

After the Rain

American Tall Tales

The Deadly Power of Medusa by Mary Pope Osborne
    and Will Osborne

Favorite Greek Myths

Favorite Medieval Tales

Favorite Norse Myths

Jason and the Argonauts by Mary Pope Osborne
    and Will Osborne
The Life of Jesus in Masterpieces of Art
Mary Pope Osborne's Tales from *The Odyssey* series
Mermaid Tales from Around the World
My Brother's Keeper
My Secret War
The Mysteries of Spider Kane
One World, Many Religions
Standing in the Light
A Time to Dance by Will Osborne and
    Mary Pope Osborne

For young-adult readers:

Haunted Waters

MARY POPE OSBORNE and NATALIE POPE BOYCE are sisters who grew up on army posts all over the world. Today, Mary lives in Connecticut. Natalie makes her home nearby in the Berkshire Hills of Massachusetts. Mary is the author of over fifty books for children. She and Natalie are currently working together on *The Random House Book of Bible Stories* and on more Magic Tree House® Research Guides.

Here's what Natalie and Mary have to say about working on *Sea Monsters:* "When we were children and lived on the ocean, we'd sometimes get stung by jellyfish. They can really sting! We'd get very cross that they dared to live in *our* ocean! Back then, we didn't know just how many animals made their homes in the sea. When we began research for this book, we got so excited. Imagine an octopus as small as a walnut or a prehistoric sea creature as big as a moving van! And guess what! We realized that the ocean doesn't belong to people; it belongs to the wonderful sea creatures that live there. We discovered that we really need to take care of these animals and their world . . . even the jellyfish!"